COUNTRIES  OF THE WORLD

GREECE

Peggy Hollinger

with photographs by Jimmy Holmes

Illustrated by Malcolm Walker

The Bookwright Press
New York • 1990

Titles in this series

Cover A busy fishing port on the Greek island of Hydra.

Opposite A small village on the hillside on the island of Symi.

© Copyright 1989 Wayland (Publishers) Ltd

First published in the United States in 1990 by
The Bookwright Press
387 Park Avenue South, New York NY 10016

First published in 1989 by Wayland (Publishers) Ltd
61 Western Road, Hove, East Sussex BN3 1JD England

Library of Congress Cataloging–in–Publication Data
Hollinger, Peggy.
    Greece / by Peggy Hollinger.
        p.   cm. — (Countries of the world)
    Bibliography: p.
    Includes index.
    Summary: Introduces the physical characteristics,
history, mythology, social life, religions, economy,
and government of Greece.
    ISBN 0–531–18305–X
    1. Greece—Juvenile literature. [1. Greece.] I. Title.
II. Series: Countries of the world (New York, N.Y.)
DF717.H65   1990
949.5—dc20   89–7375
                                         CIP
                                         AC

Typeset by Lizzie George, Wayland
Printed in Italy by G. Canale & C.S.p.A., Turin

Contents

All the words appearing in **bold** are explained in the glossary on page 46.

1 Introducing Greece

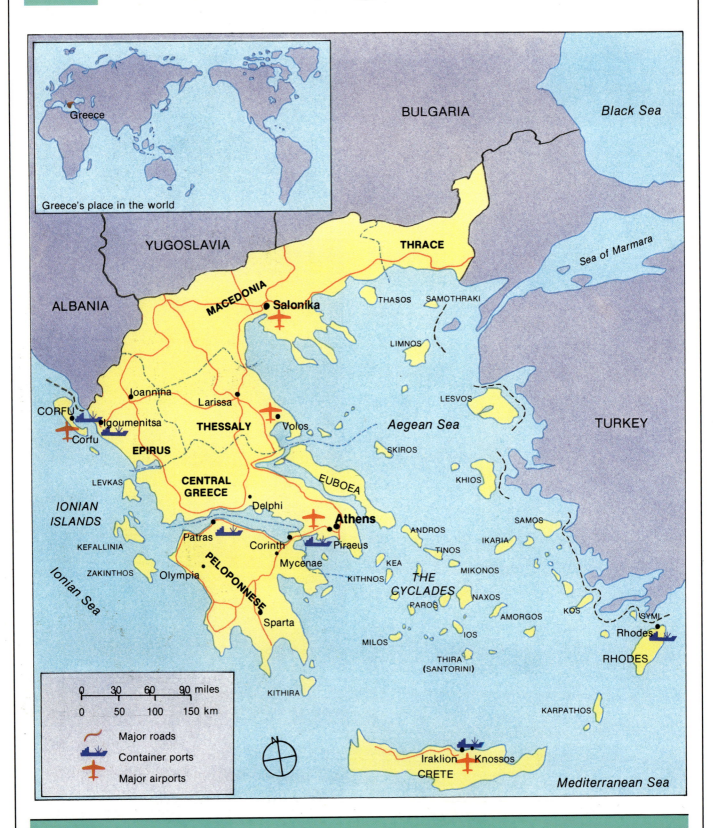

Greece's place in the world

BULGARIA

Black Sea

YUGOSLAVIA

THRACE

Sea of Marmara

ALBANIA

MACEDONIA

Salonika

THASOS   SAMOTHRAKI

LIMNOS

Ioannina

Larissa

LESVOS

CORFU

Igoumenitsa

Corfu

THESSALY

Volos

Aegean Sea

TURKEY

EPIRUS

SKIROS

*IONIAN
ISLANDS*

CENTRAL
GREECE

EUBOEA

KHIOS

SAMOS

LEVKAS

Delphi

Athens

ANDROS

IKARIA

Patras

Piraeus

KEFALLINIA

Corinth

TINOS

MIKONOS

*Ionian
Sea*

ZAKINTHOS

Mycenae

Olympia

PELOPONNESE

KEA

KITHNOS

*THE
CYCLADES*

NAXOS

KOS

Sparta

PAROS

AMORGOS

SYMI

Rhodes

MILOS

IOS

RHODES

THIRA
(SANTORINI)

KITHIRA

KARPATHOS

0	30	60	90 miles
0	50	100	150 km

Major roads

Container ports

Major airports

N

Iraklion   Knossos

CRETE

Mediterranean Sea

Greece lies in the southeast corner of Europe; its combination of mainland, **peninsula**, and thousands of islands gives the country a special character. It is a land of contrasts where ancient history meets modern living, mountains meet the sea, and East meets West.

Greece has a long, rocky coastline which extends over 1,500 km (932 mi). It is broken up by thousands of inlets and bays that run deep into the mainland. No part of Greece is further than a few hundred miles from the sea, and from a high enough vantage the sea is always in view.

Greece is sparsely populated with only 10 million people in a land of some 132,000 sq km (51,000 sq mi). Compare this to England where 49 million people live in a country of nearly the same size.

Despite its small population, Greece is determined to become a force in Western politics. It joined the **European Economic Community** (EEC) and became a full member in 1981. It has been a member

The children of Kassiopi, on Corfu, are dressed in traditional Greek costumes.

Greece	
Land area:	132,000 sq km (51,000 sq mi)
Population:	10,000,000
Capital:	Athens
Main cities:	Salonika, Iraklion, Larissa
Language:	Greek
Religion:	Greek Orthodox
Currency:	100 lepta equals one drachma

of the western military alliance, the **North Atlantic Treaty Organization** (NATO), since 1951.

The EEC has provided much money and technology to help Greece build a stronger economy and better life for its citizens. The military alliance, on the other hand, has provoked many arguments, especially over the existence of American bases in Greece. However, Greece's dispute with Turkey over land and oil rights has pushed the controversy over NATO into the background.

2 Land and climate

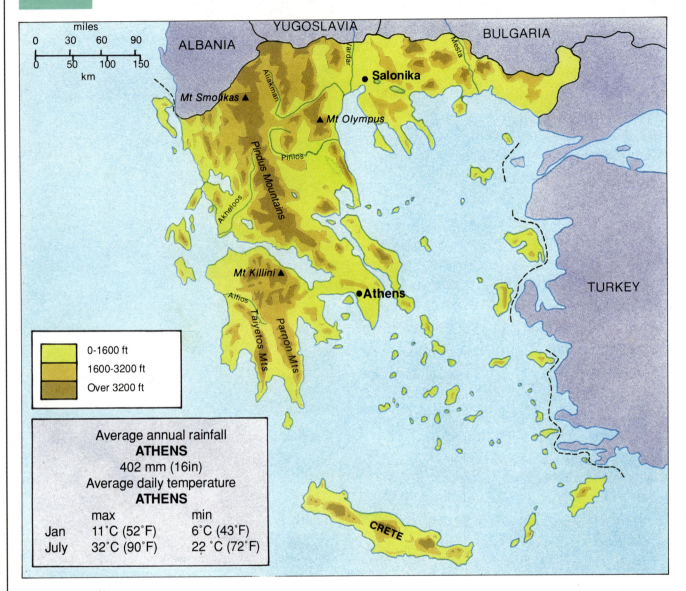

Greece is famous for its beaches and rugged coastline, but at the heart of the country is a wild and isolated mountainous region. Three-quarters of the mainland is covered by mountains which make transportation and agriculture difficult. The Greek islands are scattered across three seas – the Aegean, the Ionian, and the Mediterranean. The islands are really the peaks of mountains that once belonged to the ranges covering the mainland. The mountain tops became islands thousands of years ago when the Mediterranean basin flooded with water.

Greece's most famous mountain is Mount Olympus, in **mythology** the home of the gods of ancient Greece. It is also the highest mountain, rising to 2,917 m (9,750 ft). The Pindus range of mountains runs like a backbone down the center of mainland Greece. The upper slopes of its high peaks are covered with fir and pine forests.

The climate of the inland mountain regions varies sharply from the coastal or island climates. Greece has a unique combination of European and Mediterranean climates. A European climate has hot, muggy summers and cold, snowy winters. The Mediterranean climate gets warm, wet winters and hot, dry summers. Much of Greece is a hot, dry place where the sun shines most of the year. Yet the mountains can be covered with snow until June.

Above Snow lies on the Gamila Peaks of the Pindus mountains even in the middle of June.

Below Corfu, Greece's most northerly island, is also the greenest.

3 Wildlife and plants

In Greece, vegetation and wildlife survive in unfriendly conditions. The weather is usually hot and dry and the soil is poor and rocky. To cope with the harsh conditions, many plants have developed protective characteristics. Orange and lemon trees, for instance, have waxy leaves which resist the heat and retain moisture.

Like the climate, Greece's **flora** and **fauna** are a combination of European and Mediterranean species. Common flowers in the north, where the weather is more European, are the iris, crocus and tulip. In southern Greece, where the weather is hotter and drier, Mediterranean flowers such as the narcissus, water lily and chamomile grow.

Nature was very important to the ancient Greeks. It played a major role in their folklore and mythology. Unfortunately, it has received less attention in modern Greece. The idea of **conservation** did not take hold until after World War II (1939-45), when the government set up several programs to plant trees on barren hills and in the cities.

Protecting sea life has also become important. This is because industrial **pollution** is taking its toll of Greece's rich sea life. Scientists have estimated that 246 species of fish inhabit Greek waters. They include lobster, shrimp, crab and the

The goat is commonly seen in Greece and valued for its meat and rich milk.

playful dolphin. The government has plans for several conservation projects for sea life. Sea parks have already been created to protect turtles and seals.

Greece's national forest service has also set aside parks where birdwatchers can go to spot some of the 358 different species said to inhabit the country. These include birds of prey such as eagles, hawks and vultures, as well as pelicans, pheasants, storks and nightingales.

Wild animals are rarely seen in Greece. Thousands of years of hunting have taken their toll. Yet many different kinds of animals are native to the country, including boar, brown bears, lynx, deer, wolves, jackals, porcupines and badgers. There are also animals that live only in Greece. The rare white agrimi goat is a domestic animal that is found mainly on the island of Crete.

Above Wild flowers make a colorful pattern on the hills and fields in springtime.

Left The European lynx makes its home in the forested regions of the country but is rarely seen.

4 Ancient history

The ancient palace of Knossos on Crete was discovered and restored by archaeologists.

The first Greeks are believed to have been invaders from the north, in about 3,000 BC. They swept down across the southern peninsula and conquered the tribespeople called the Aegeans. The invaders did not reach Crete, and it was here that a civilization of incredible richness was able to flourish until about 1,400 BC.

The people of Crete were known as the Minoans. They lived in big, beautiful cities and were ruled by a priest-king. They were a peaceful people and traded with other countries.

Archaeologists have discovered evidence showing that the Minoans had modern comforts long before their northern European neighbors. In the king's palace at Knossos, modern bathroom systems with bathtubs, hot and cold water, and flush toilets have been discovered.

The Minoan civilization came to a violent end in 1,400 BC. A volcanic explosion on the nearby island of Santorini is believed to have created tidal waves and earthquakes that set off the destruction of the Minoan kingdom. It was eventually invaded by people from the north, and the palace at Knossos was sacked and burned. The mainland of Greece then became the major Mediterranean sea power.

It was after 1,200 BC that Greeks began to form the city-state, or "polis," as it was known. These were **independent** cities with their own rulers, armies and governments. The many city-states developed different types of government, and it is here that democracy (or government by popular vote) was first practiced.

The fifth century BC is known as the classical period, when Greece led the world in the sciences, culture and the arts. It was also a violent time, when the city-states fought wars among themselves. These wars weakened the country, and Greece was conquered by Philip of **Macedonia** in 338 BC. His son, Alexander the Great, extended his father's empire and took Greek culture to the lands he conquered.

However, just 145 years before Christ, the Romans invaded and conquered the Greek empire. For the next 2,000 years, Greece was governed by foreign rulers: Romans, Byzantines, and finally, the Ottoman Turks until 1829.

Above The Parthenon, the main temple on the Acropolis was built from 448 to 438 BC.

Below A carving on an ancient tomb shows Alexander the Great leading a hunt.

Important dates

6000 BC	Aegeans arrive in Crete.
3500 BC	Invaders conquer Crete.
1400 BC	Minoan civilization destroyed.
1200 BC	Development of city-states.
546 BC	Persians conquer much of Greece.
480 BC	Greek cities defeat Persians at sea. Athens becomes the head of a group of cities known as the Delian League, formed to protect the mainland from overseas invaders.
431-404 BC	War between the city-states, known as the Peloponnesian War. Athens loses to Sparta.
338 BC	Philip II of Macedonia conquers Greece.
145 BC	Romans invade and conquer the Greek Empire.
AD 330	Greece comes under Byzantine rule.
1452-1821	Greece under Turkish rule.

5 Modern history

The war for independence from Turkey lasted nine years, although there had been minor rebellions on and off for hundreds of years.

Greece's fight for freedom was closely watched in Europe. The "London Protocol" was a treaty which established a Greek nation in 1830. It set up a **constitutional monarchy** and appointed the German, Otto of Bavaria, as king of Greece. The Greeks did not like this very much and **civil war** continued to plague the country. After a series of political shake-ups, and a failed attempt to set up a **republic**, the military **dictator** Ioannis Metaxas seized power in 1935. He ruled until Italy invaded Greece during World War II.

Greece was occupied by hostile countries until 1945. During this

King Constantine surrounded by the military leaders who overthrew his government in 1967.

time, many Greeks were killed in the **resistance** and entire villages were wiped out by the occupiers. Most of the population lived on the edge of starvation as their farms were destroyed and food was hard to find.

After the war, Greece was again torn by civil war. The country did not have a stable government for another twenty years.

In 1967 a group of **military** colonels overthrew the government headed by 27-year-old King Constantine and abolished the parliament. The colonels ruled for seven years. It was a hard time for the Greek people. Political differences were not allowed, and the colonels kept strict control over television, radio and newspapers.

In 1974 tensions with Turkey, never completely relaxed since independence, flared again. An attempted military **coup** on nearby Cyprus aroused fears in Turkey that Greece was about to take over the island. Turkey invaded Cyprus, saying it was protecting the Turks who lived there.

German paratroopers land on Crete in the invasion which devastated the island during World War II.

The military government could not lead the country through the crisis, and the politician Constantine Caramanlis was recalled from Paris where he had fled during the rule of the colonels. He formed a **parliamentary government**, which is the basis of the Greek system today.

Important dates

1821-30	War of independence from Turkey.
1830	Greece wins independence from Turkey. London Protocol sets up a constitutional monarchy.
1935	Military dictator Ioannis Metaxas seizes power.
1941	Germany invades and occupies Greece during World War II.
1945	End of war and liberation of Greece.
1967	Military coup and the rule of the colonels begins.
1974	Turkey invades Cyprus.

6 Mythology

Traditional Greek vases. The Greek hero Hercules is depicted at the top of the central vase.

The ancient Greeks worshiped many gods and goddesses. Their religious world was peopled with all sorts of fantastic beings who often played a part in their daily lives. Their adventures make up the collection of tales we know as the Greek myths.

But myths are more than just religious stories. The Greek myths told tales about the world in which the Greeks lived and explained how things happened in the world.

Mythology also provided entertainment for the Greeks. The blind poet Homer who lived about 800 BC, collected these stories together for the first time in his books, the *Iliad* and the *Odyssey*.

Mount Olympus was the legendary home of the gods. The most important god was Zeus. He carried a thunderbolt and ruled over the other gods and goddesses. His wife Hera was the **patron** goddess of marriage and childbirth.

There were hundreds of other **deities**. Athena was the goddess of wisdom and war. Poseidon was the god of the sea, Ares the god of war, Artemis the goddess of hunting, and her brother Apollo the god of music. The world of the gods also included centaurs – half-man, half-horse – dryads, or forest fairies, naiads or water sprites, and the satyr, half-man, half-goat.

Many plants and trees are connected with humans or minor gods who fell out of favor with the greater Olympians. The laurel tree, according to legend, was once the nymph Daphne who was changed into a tree so she could escape from the god Apollo. Because he loved the nymph, he is usually shown with a crown of laurel leaves which he wears in her memory.

At this temple at Delphi there was a shrine where the ancient Greeks consulted the god Apollo.

7 The people today

Left Village women take a break in the shade with their knitting after the morning's work is done.

Below Traditional dress is still worn in many parts of Greece. These men are wearing the costumes of the Cyclades islands.

Greeks have always been a very **patriotic** people. Politics play a very important part in their lives, probably because Greeks fought for so many years to have their own government.

There are very few **immigrants** in Greece. After the Russian Revolution (1917), some Russians **emigrated** to Greece, probably drawn by religious ties with the Orthodox Church. But they were few, and their descendants have largely mixed in with the Greek population. There is also a Greek-Turkish community which remains from the days of the Ottoman occupation. But this community is also small, making up less than one in a hundred of the general population.

Greece has a long tradition of emigration and since joining the EEC this has increased. It is now easier for Greeks to settle and work in other parts of Europe, where they are likely to find better-paid jobs. Many Greeks leave the country for a while, but when they have saved enough money they return and set up a business or buy some land.

For those who remain there is a sharp division between country and city, mainland and island. People in the country are usually farmers who spend more time at home. Schools are small and the communities are very close-knit.

In the cities, life is much faster. Schools are bigger and people live in smaller homes, usually apartments.

People on the islands lead a very quiet life in the winter. They might not work during these months, since the weather is too poor for fishing and all the tourists have gone home. Many island people go back to the mainland for the winter, where they may have another business, and return to the islands again in time for the tourist season.

Greeks often do their shopping from these traveling stores. Melons are weighed and sold from the back of a van in Athens.

8 Cities

Athens, once a small village, is now a sprawling city of 3.2 million people.

Athens is the capital of Greece. It is here that the ancient Greeks built their main temples to the gods on top of a steep hill called the Acropolis. This means the "upper city." On the slope of the Acropolis stands an ancient theater which is still used for plays today.

The modern city of Athens sprawls out from the Acropolis along a valley basin. When it was named as the capital in 1834, Athens was only a tiny village. After World War II it was developed as an industrial base and grew to be a busy center. Today more than 3 million people live in and around the city. This is about a quarter of the total population of Greece.

This rapid growth has created many problems for the city's inhabitants. In the 1960s apartments and office buildings were built to cope with the booming population, but they were built in a hurry and without much planning. They are very tall and close together, making the city appear very crowded.

To make matters worse, there are few green, open spaces in the city. Officials are trying to control the pollution from cars and factories. Trees are being planted beside the roads in the hope they will make the city more attractive. Private cars are restricted in the city center on weekdays to try to lessen the smog they cause.

Salonika is Greece's second largest city. More than 800,000 people live in this northern seaport city. Salonika is an industrial city, and a center for business and finance.

There are few other cities like Salonika and Athens in Greece. Large towns include Iraklion, on the island of Crete, and Larissa on the mainland.

Left Salonika, the country's second largest city and capital of northern Greece, is an important international port.

Below Shopping arcades such as this one in Athens are a familiar sight in Greek cities.

9 Family life

Family life is very important to Greeks. Even when children grow up and leave home, they return to their families for holidays and celebrations.

In the city, most families live in apartments. A typical one may have two bedrooms and children share one. Most families in the country have their own house, but it is not much bigger than a city apartment.

Most city families tend to be small, usually with two children. The average family in the country, however, might have three children. Greeks do not think of the family as just the mother, father and children. Families include the grandmothers, grandfathers, aunts, uncles and cousins. So a family reunion in a Greek village is a big, noisy and happy affair.

Families who have gone to the cities in search of work will reunite in their home village for their vacations. August is the vacation month and cities practically close down, as most Greeks have returned to the villages or islands for family reunions. Most city families with roots in the country own a summer home in their village.

Three generations of a family share a watermelon outside.

Left Family ties are strong and children are taught to take care of their younger sisters and brothers.

Below A young boy helps to process tobacco leaves grown on the family farm.

Above A grandmother takes care of her grandchild while the parents work.

Several generations often live in the same house, especially in families where both parents work. This is happening more and more as Greeks expect a higher standard of living. It is not unusual for one parent to have two jobs. Both parents are usually able to work because of the number of low-cost nurseries, which have been set up by the government to look after children during the day.

In the country, both parents work on the farm, and it is more common to have the grandparents working and living with the family. Children also help on the farm after school and on weekends. If a family owns a business, the children are expected to help there too.

Although the legal age for employment is 16 years, Greek parents do not expect their children to work at a job while they are at secondary school or at college. Most parents believe that students should enjoy themselves before beginning careers. So parents provide them with spending money, and few young people leave home before they start working or get married.

10 Education

Education is very important to the Greeks. These primary school children are expected to work hard at their lessons.

Education is very important to the Greeks. For many years Greece had few schools and even fewer universities. Today, however, as Greeks earn more money and improve their standard of living, parents are more anxious for their children to go through secondary school.

Greek schools are very strict. Students are expected to read and write correctly by the age of eight. They go to school from 8:30 a.m. to 2:30 p.m. and often have a lot of homework. The usual subjects studied are geography, math, history, modern Greek, and religion. Only students who are not Greek Orthodox are exempt from the religion course.

There is no lunch during the school day, but students are allowed a ten minute break every hour. After school, children go home for their lunch, which is a big, cooked meal.

All levels of education are paid for by the state, and children must attend school until the age of 15. There are three stages of school before college: elementary school from 6 to 12 years old; secondary school from 12 to 15 years old; and lyceum, the **optional** stage before college, from 15 to 18 years old.

On the islands, these stages are often mixed, as there may be only one school for the community. So students of all ages and levels may study in the same classroom with the same teacher.

Students who go to the lyceum often attend a private "cramming school" for three to four hours in the

Schools, colleges and universities

Preschool and elementary schools: 14,393 (1,066,581 pupils)

Secondary schools: 3,214 (803,269 pupils)

Higher education colleges and universities: 102 (14 universities) (167,957 students)

Above The children take a break from their classes in the school playground.

Right The University of Ioannia is one of several new universities in Greece.

afternoon. This is paid for by the parents and teaches a variety of subjects including languages, music and technical subjects to prepare the student for the college entrance examination.

There are 14 universities in Greece and the competition for places is strong. Many students travel abroad to study, as the subjects at Greek universities are limited. Since joining the EEC in 1981, this has become easier and cheaper for Greek students.

11 Sports and leisure

Greece's tradition in sports goes back thousands of years. Ancient Greeks were proud of their athletic skills and started the Olympic Games in 776 BC. The games were originally part of a religious festival dedicated to the god Zeus. They were eventually abolished in AD 394 when they became corrupt, but they were revived 1,500 years later in 1896.

They are still held in different countries every four years. In ancient times, all wars were stopped for as long as the games lasted. The champion of the games won no prize but was crowned with a wreath of olive leaves as a token of honor.

Above Greek waters are ideal for diving and snorkeling.

Left Basketball is very popular in Greece.

An opening ceremony at Athens Olympic Stadium in September 1982.

Today Greece's sports tradition is carried on in schools and sports clubs. As Greece becomes more prosperous, more local councils are building sports centers for public use.

The most popular sports are basketball, soccer, and volleyball. Basketball became a national passion when Greece won the world championships in 1987. Now basketball teams are springing up all over the country. Soccer is also followed with enthusiasm, although Greece has not yet won a world championship.

The main sports arena is the Olympic Stadium in Athens. It was completed in 1982 and seats 80,000 people. Soccer matches and track events are held there, drawing competitors from all over the world. In recent years more than 40 sports stadiums have been built around the country in an effort to attract more international competitions.

Automobile racing is a favorite sport. The Acropolis Rally draws thousands of people every year and auto racing is popular on the islands.

Swimming is, of course, very popular in Greece. Most children learn to swim when they are very young. Sailing, diving, tennis and golf are other popular sports, and the traditionally English game of cricket is even played on the island of Corfu.

12 Shopping

An average Greek family shops once or twice a week. Most stores are still owned and run by a family. They are usually small shops with a little bit of everything for sale – paper, household goods, sometimes even clothes.

Supermarkets are becoming more common, especially in the cities, but people prefer to buy from the smaller shops and markets. Bread, rolls and cookies are bought from bakeries where the oven is often in full view of the customers. In the rural villages the baker's oven may be situated outside in a courtyard and is the focal point of daily life. Bread is sold by weight, as are sugar, cheese, olives and spices in other stores

Another favorite way to shop is at the markets. Greeks like to see,

Left A cluttered market stand in Athens sells a wide variety of foods.

Below Fresh bread is very important to Greeks, who usually go to their local bakery every day.

Above Fresh seafood is sold in fish markets, and includes specialties such as octopus.

examine and choose what they are buying. The market stalls are piled high with fresh vegetables, cheese, meat and herbs. There are huge vats of black and green olives and a variety of dried peas and beans, rice and flour. In the meat markets there is a variety of fresh meat and game birds and also plenty of stalls selling fresh fish. The market stalls also have goods such as shoes and clothes for sale, and these are often cheaper than in the stores.

Kiosks are very popular in the towns and villages in Greece. In the main towns they are located on virtually every street corner. A kiosk is a booth which sells many small items such as stamps, pens, confectionery and cards. It is also often an information bureau, and may have a public telephone. Many kiosks stay open all day and night. In the villages kiosks are favorite places for people to meet for a chat.

In the more remote areas of Greece most produce is bought from street vendors. Fishmongers and fruit and vegetable sellers travel along the narrow roads in open-backed trucks or vans. They stop at each street and using a loudspeaker call to everyone what goods are for sale.

Kiosks like this one are small shops which can be found on almost every street corner.

13 Food

Greek cooking tends to be very seasonal with an emphasis on fresh food at every meal. Breakfast is generally very light – for many Greeks it is just a cup of coffee. Otherwise it may consist of fresh fruit, bread and cheese, and sheep's milk yogurt with honey. Lunch, the main meal, is usually eaten at home between 12:00 and 3:00 p.m. In rural communities there is often an afternoon rest at home, during which time schools and businesses close.

Supper is a light meal eaten in the late evening. However, people working in towns may have a light lunch and a main meal between 8:00 p.m. and 10:00 p.m.

Above *A family eating outside a taverna, where the food is fresh and inexpensive.*

Left *A colorful selection of Greek dishes.*

During the day tavernas are used as outdoor cafés where busy shoppers buy refreshments.

Greeks often go out for dinner, usually to a taverna. This is a small cheap restaurant where customers go into the kitchen and choose their meal by looking at what is cooking. If a friend is invited for dinner, it will probably be a meal at a taverna and not at home.

Greek food makes good use of the country's abundance of vegetables and seafood. Greece is not a great meat-eating country, but the most popular meat is lamb. Souvlakia is marinated meat on a skewer, like kebabs. It is often broiled or grilled over charcoal.

Fish is part of the staple diet. It is often mixed with vegetables and baked or cooked over charcoal. Red mullet and fried squid are common foods in Greece.

The Greeks cook main dishes using a variety of vegetables. The most popular are eggplant, zucchini, spinach, okra, artichokes and root vegetables. They are cooked in a variety of ways, often stuffed, to make a tasty meal.

A Greek salad may be eaten with any meal. It is made from goat's cheese, tomatoes, olives and lettuce, dressed with olive oil or lemon and vinegar.

The Greeks are also very fond of sweet desserts which are usually made with nuts, spices and honey.

14 Religion

*A Greek Orthodox priest stands in front of a panel of holy pictures which shields the altar. Icons of Jesus (**inset**), Mary and the saints decorate the walls of Greek churches.*

Greek or Eastern Orthodox, a form of Christianity, is the main religion. Almost all of the population belongs to the Orthodox faith. The word Orthodox comes from the Greek word meaning "right-believing."

Members of the Greek Orthodox Church go to a service on Sunday that can last up to three hours. In the more traditional churches and often in the villages, men stay on one side of the church and women on the other. Most people stand for the whole three hours.

The entire service is chanted, and much of it takes place behind a screen which surrounds the altar. As the mass continues, many people walk around the church to kiss the icons, or holy pictures. These are paintings of Jesus, Mary and the saints. There are no statues in a Greek Orthodox church.

Greek Orthodox priests wear colorful robes for the church service, but normally they wear long black cassocks and tall round hats. They do not shave or cut their hair, which is tied up in a small bun at the back.

Priests can be married, but bishops and other higher-ranking clergy must be single.

The Greek Orthodox Church does not have a Pope like the Catholic Church. Instead, it has a **Patriarch** who is based in Istanbul in Turkey. The Patriarch dictates the religious laws of the faith.

Monasteries are very important to the Orthodox faith. They are scattered throughout the mainland and the islands, often in very remote places. Mount Athos is a famous location of 20 monasteries and has been granted a special independent status from Greece. No women, or even female animals, are allowed to visit the monastery-state.

Above right Roadside shrines often mark the scenes of accidents in the countryside.

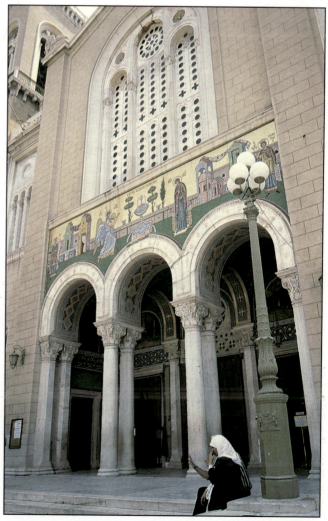

Right A woman sits outside a modern Greek Orthodox cathedral which is decorated with intricate mosaics.

15 Festivals

Rarely a day goes by in Greece without some kind of celebration.

Easter is the biggest holiday and the most important festival. This is traditionally the time when families reunite in their home town. They will celebrate with a special feast, usually lamb roasted on a **spit**, and special church services.

The celebrations go on for days. In some villages they last 40 days, until Ascension Day. Schoolchildren have 15 days' holiday and are given presents of new clothes on Easter Sunday. This holiday marks the end of winter and the beginning of the warmer months.

A carnival celebrates the beginning of Lent, the 40 days leading up to Easter. Greek children dress up in costumes and visit friends. They wear the costumes to school and sing special carnival songs. Parades with floats and bands are held in the cities.

Above A woman ties a carnation to a shrine on Good Friday, the beginning of the Easter festival.

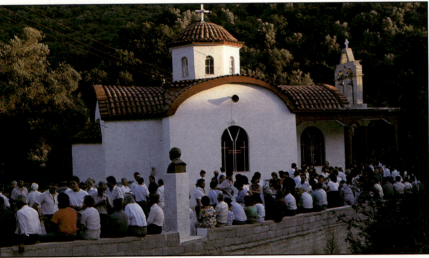

Left Village weddings are usually an occasion for the entire town to gather for a celebration.

Village women dress in traditional costume for the Easter procession.

Birthdays are not as important as they are in other countries. Children and adults celebrate "name days" instead. This is the day dedicated to the saint after whom the person is named. On this day people celebrating the name day take presents, such as sweet cakes, to friends. They also receive presents, and a special church service is held for all the people celebrating their name day in the same village. Villages often have their own name days and the whole village celebrates with food, music and dancing. The church bells ring all day to let the surrounding villages know there is a festival going on.

Families reunite at Christmas, but this is more a religious holiday than a time for presents. Gift-giving happens on Agios Vassilis Day, or the feast of Saint Basil. A special cake called Saint Basil's cake is served after dinner. Baked into the cake is a small coin, and whoever finds the coin is said to have good luck for the next year.

Other holidays are Independence Day on March 25, celebrated with fireworks, and "Ohi Day" on October 28. Ohi means "no" in Greek and this marks the day in 1940 that the Greek prime minister told Italy's dictator, Benito Mussolini, that his troops could not enter Greece.

16 Culture and the arts

Oedipus Rex, *the story of a mythological king, as performed by the Greek National Theater company.*

Greeks are famous for their strong, energetic dancing. They are proud of their national music and their dancing skills. They will dance at weddings and festivals, and even in the tavernas, after a long, relaxed evening meal.

There are two basic kinds of national dancing – fast dances, like the Syrtaki, and slow ones like the Tsamikos. Fast dances express happy feelings and are usually danced by men. They have intricate footwork and include high leaps in the air. The slow dances usually tell a tragic story and are often danced alone. In competitions and festivals, dancers wear national costumes. The men wear pleated skirts, shirts with large sleeves, a **bolero** and a tassled hat. The women wear long, full skirts and baggy shirts.

Greeks are also proud of their ancient culture. Hippocrates, a famous doctor in ancient Greece, set up a school of medicine on the island of Kos. He made his students take an oath to care for people that is still sworn by doctors today. Ancient Greek poets and dramatists such as Homer, Sophocles, and Sappho, are still read and studied around the world, as are philosophers such as Plato and Aristotle.

Modern Greek writers are also considered to be some of the best in the world. The Cretan writer Nikos Kazantzakis wrote the well-known book *Zorba the Greek*, which was made into a movie.

Modern Greek culture is vibrant, too. Composers like Vangelis and the singer Nana Mouskouri have won international recognition. In bars or in nightclubs, Greeks might show their appreciation of a good singer by throwing plates at the singer's feet. The better the singer, the less he or she will move as the plates crash on the stage.

Greeks are also famous for their handicrafts. Hand-painted pottery, delicately embroidered clothing, jewelry, and leather bags, shoes and accessories can be found in any part of Greece.

Above *A wood carver carves an intricate screen to surround a church altar.*

A pottery shop displays its wares. Greek pottery is based on designs known in the country for thousands of years.

Farming and fishing

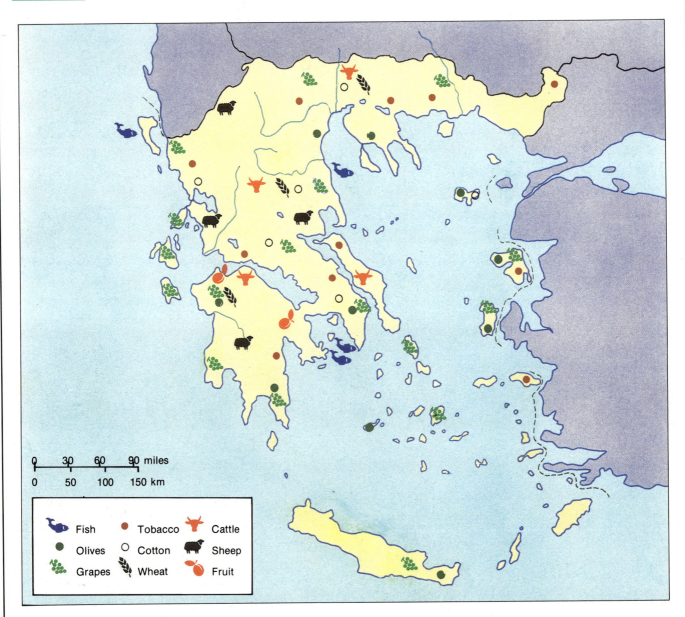

	Fish		Tobacco		Cattle
	Olives		Cotton		Sheep
	Grapes		Wheat		Fruit

Although Greece is mainly an agricultural country, there is actually very little good land for farming. Less than a third of the land can be farmed because of the mountains that cover most of the country. The main agricultural region of Greece is the fertile plains area of Thrace, east of the Pindus mountain range.

Until very recently, agriculture was the biggest money earner in Greece. Sugar and wheat are the country's main **commercial** products, but other crops are tobacco, cotton, corn, lemons, oranges, olives, figs, and almonds. Crete is famous for its sultana raisins.

Much of Greece's agricultural potential has been wasted because of outdated farming techniques. Most farms are small (about 7 ½ acres) which makes it difficult to grow the quantity of crops needed for export.

Every member of the family works on the farm, and it is not unusual to see very old men and women working in the fields. About one-third of the Greek population works on farms.

The government is now trying to modernize farming techniques and encourage specialized agriculture, which is more productive for **export**.

Fishermen on the island of Levras carefully put away their nets after the morning's catch.

This will help Greece bring money into the country. The government is also trying to increase the amount of land which can be used for farming by draining marsh areas.

Fishing is a big industry. About 50,000 people work on fishing boats or in the factories where fish are processed and canned. Surprisingly, for a country with such a rich natural resource, Greece still imports many fish products.

Sponge fishing was once an important branch of the fishing industry and employed many people on the islands. It is dying out, however, as most people are buying the cheaper, man-made sponges.

18 Industry

Greece has few natural resources, so industry has been slow to develop. Since World War II, however, the country has made special efforts to encourage new industries such as **food processing**. Most industry is based in Athens and Salonika.

Traditionally, industries in Greece are small and family owned. Shipping and ship building are exceptions, however. The Greek **merchant fleet** is the sixth largest in the world, and some of the world's richest people are Greek ship owners.

In the 1960s these ship owners were encouraged to invest in Greek industry. This resulted in a boom in the mining industry, energy, communications and financial services.

| Main exports: | Tobacco, olives, wheat, cotton, sultana raisins |
| Main imports: | Machinery, transportation equipment |

Above Cement is used in almost all Greek building projects. It is processed at places such as this cement works near Athens.

Left Huge tankers dock for repairs at the shipyard at Eleusis.

Above The golden beaches and warm climate draw thousands of tourists and a large amount of money to Greece every year.

Right Greece is famous for its cheap, handmade leather goods.

Government agricultural programs in the 1950s and 1960s boosted tobacco, cotton and wheat production, resulting in the growth of the cigarette and textile industries.

Tourism is one of the biggest money-earning industries in Greece. About eight million people visit Greece every year. Hotels, restaurants and transportation services have sprung up to cater to the growing number of visitors.

Tourists and the money they spend are largely responsible for the higher wages earned by most Greeks today. Unfortunately these same tourists are spoiling the environment, and making it difficult for cottage industries to be run from the home.

Greece's most **unexploited** resource is water. The government is trying to encourage the use of **hydroelectric power**, but it is still an underdeveloped industry.

19 Transportation

Left Electric trolleys crisscross the city of Athens. These buses are quiet and create virtually no pollution.

Below The donkey is still used for transportation on rocky Greek roads.

The most common means of transportation in Greece is the bus. Each province runs its own bus system. In the country a bus is usually crowded and looks something like an old school bus, with a radio blaring away at the front. It is the only way to travel from village to village, especially in the mountains, other than private car. Buses travel on narrow roads that wind along steep cliffs unprotected by barriers.

Most of the roads are unpaved and rough, although there are three modern highways, which cross the country. The government is trying to improve the road system, but it will be many years before Greek roads are completely modernized.

Railroads were not begun until the late nineteenth century – very late by European standards. They are owned and run by the state, but few people use them as they are not extensive and are very slow. The government is also trying to improve the railroad system.

Most Greek families own a car – usually just one, as cars are very expensive. The legal age for driving is 18. Most cars are imported and are heavily taxed.

The most important method of traveling in Greece is by sea. Ferries, steamers, and boats called caïques, are used to go from island to island or between the mainland and the islands. Caïques are small boats, pointed at each end, which are usually run as an informal ferry service by a family.

Greece also has its own international airline. Olympic Airways flies between islands, to and from the mainland and to many cities around the world. The airline, like the railroads, is state-owned.

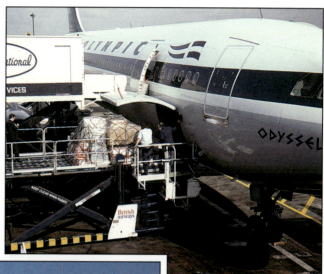

Above It is possible to travel to most parts of the country on the state-run airline, Olympic Airways.

Left Because Greece has thousands of islands, ferries and steamers are a vital method of transportation.

20 Government

Greece has been a democratic republic since 1974. This means the people choose representatives to govern the country. In 1974 Greeks voted to reject a **monarchy** and adopted a constitution which set up a parliamentary democracy.

The parliament is made up of 300 deputies elected to office for a four-year term. The parliament elects a president who holds office for five years. The head of the party that wins the most seats in parliament is appointed prime minister by the president.

Andreas Papandreou is the leader of the Pasok Party and the Prime Minister of Greece.

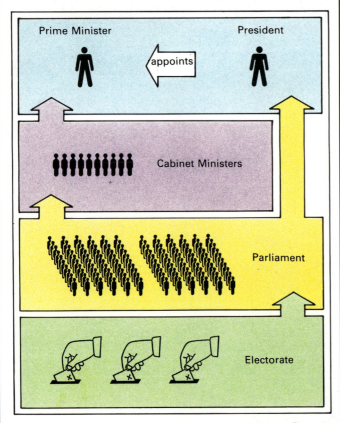

A diagram showing the structure of the Greek government.

Today the Pasok **Socialist** Party holds power in Greece. Since 1981, when Pasok won power, many changes have been made. The voting age was lowered to 18, women were made equal to men under the law, and civil marriage was made legal.

The police force has also been strengthened. Until recently, there were two police forces, one for the country and one for the city. Now the two have been combined, making the administration of the force easier and more efficient.

There is still a special force called the tourist police, however. It is based in the resorts and popular tourist spots to deal with problems having to do with foreign visitors.

Important dates

1944	Rebellion by communist-led groups. Beginning of a civil war between communist groups and royalists, who backed a constitutional monarchy.	1974	Colonels fail to lead Greece through the crisis sparked by the invasion of Cyprus. Constantine Caramanlis is called out of exile to set up a democratic republic.
1949	Civil war ends.	1975	New constitution of the Republic of Greece is approved.
1951	Greece joins NATO military alliance.	1981	Pasok Socialist Party is elected to power. Andreas Papandreou becomes prime minister. Greece becomes a full member of the EEC.
1967-74	The military dictatorship, known as the rule of the colonels. Television, radio and newspaper censorship was practiced during this time.	1989	General election scheduled for June, 1989.

Every member of this force must speak at least one foreign language.

The divided island of Cyprus poses special problems for the Greek government. It is important to Greece, because it lies just off the coast of Turkey and has rich oil potential. The southern half of Cyprus is guarded by a special Greek force, while the northern half is occupied by Turkish troops. Greek Cypriots elect their own president and parliament in the southern part of the island, and the Turkish Cypriots vote for a different government in the north.

Greece recognizes Cyprus as an independent state and has a **diplomatic mission** on the island. It does not recognize the government elected by the Turkish Cypriots in the north. Cyprus has become a rallying point for Greek patriotism which demands that the island be united under Greek rule.

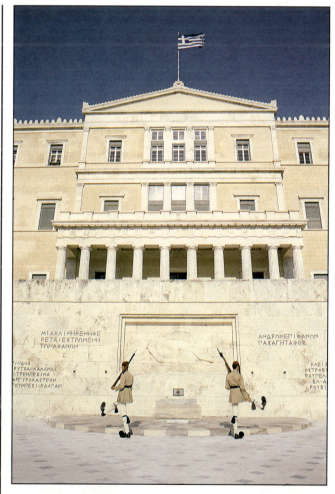

Evzones, soldiers in traditional dress, guard state buildings.

21 Facing the future

After hundreds of years of occupation, civil war and severe poverty for its people, Greece is finally beginning to achieve real progress.

There is little unemployment in Greece and wages are better than ever before. Everyone is entitled to a free education, and EEC grants and loans have helped Greece build hospitals and schools, and improve roads, agriculture and industry.

Yet Greece still faces some difficult problems in the future. As young people become better educated, they will expect to have more opportunities in their own country. At the moment many have to leave Greece to find the kinds of jobs they are looking for, jobs in scientific research, for example.

When these boys are old enough to work, there will be more job opportunities in Greece.

Greece also faces some very tough political problems. The Cyprus issue must be resolved if Greece is to escape the threat of war that remains while the island is divided. Prime Minister Andreas Papandreou appears to be determined to come to terms with this problem and has held talks with Turkish President Turgut Ozal to try to find a solution.

Greece's biggest problem is how to build up industry and give Greeks the opportunities they deserve without destroying the environment, traditions and culture that have been a source of Greek pride for centuries.

President Ozal of Turkey (center) shakes the hand of Greek Prime Minister Papandreou.

Greeks often gather in cafés such as this one in Athens for a chat, perhaps about their hopes for the future.

Glossary

Archaeologists People who study history by digging up the remains of ancient sites.

Bolero A loose, waist-length jacket.

Civil war A war between people living in the same country.

Commercial Having to do with goods that are bought and sold.

Conservation Preservation and protection of the natural environment.

Constitutional monarchy A government in which the rights and powers of the monarch are controlled by parliament.

Coup A successful uprising or action.

Deity A god or goddess.

Dictator A ruler who has total power over a country.

Diplomatic mission A group of people who represent one country in another (as Greece in Cyprus, for example).

Emigrate To leave one country to live permanently in another.

European Economic Community (EEC) Also called the Common Market, this is a group of twelve countries that try to coordinate policies on agriculture, industry, trade and taxes.

Export To send goods out of the country for sale abroad.

Fauna The animals of a region.

Flora The plants of a region.

Food processing Making raw foods into finished products that may be canned or packaged.

Hydroelectric power Producing energy from water power.

Immigrants People who come to live in a new country.

Independent Self-governing and not ruled by others (as "an independent state").

Macedonia Ancient kingdom located on the northeast part of the Greek peninsula.

Merchant fleet A fleet of ships that can be hired to carry goods.

Military To do with soldiers, weapons or warfare.

Monarchy A nation with a king or queen as head of state.

Mythology The ancient stories about gods, heroes or supernatural happenings of a particular culture.

North Atlantic Treaty Organization (NATO) An international military alliance, which is made up of sixteen countries.

Optional Something left to personal choice rather than forced or required.

Parliamentary government A country governed by an elected body of representatives called a parliament.

Patriarch Leader of the Greek Orthodox faith, similar to a bishop.

Patriotic Strongly supporting one's own country and its way of life.

Patron saint A saint regarded as the guardian of some person, place or event.

Peninsula A narrow strip of land jutting out from the mainland into the sea.

Pollution The release of substances into the air, water or land that may upset the natural balance of the environment.

Republic A form of government without a monarch, usually headed by a president.

Resistance An organization that opposes and fights an enemy for national freedom.

Socialist A person who believes that land, transportation, natural resources and major industries should be owned and operated by the state.

Spit A long, thin metal spike to hold meat while it is being roasted.

Unexploited Not used to full advantage (as "an unexploited resource").

Books to read

Elliott, Drossoula V. & Elliott, Sloane. *We Live in Greece* (Bookwright, 1984).

Gay, Kathlyn. *Science in Ancient Greece* (Franklin Watts, 1988).

Harris, Nathaniel. *Alexander the Great and the Greeks* (Bookwright, 1986).

Horton, Casey. *Ancient Greeks,* Rev. Edition (Gloucester, 1984).

Powell, Anton. *The Greek World* (Franklin Watts, 1987).

Robinson, Charles Alexander. *Ancient Greece,* Rev. Edition (Franklin Watts, 1984).

Rousou, Maria. *I am a Greek Orthodox* (Franklin Watts, 1987).

Rutland, Jonathan. *See Inside an Ancient Greek Town* (Warwick, 1986).

Picture acknowledgments

All photographs were taken by Jimmy Holmes with the exception of the following: All-sport (UK) Ltd 25; Cephas Picture Library 16 (bottom), 21 (middle); Chapel Studios 7 (bottom), 9 (right), 37; Bruce Coleman 9 (left), 15, 32 (top), 33, 34 (top); Greg Evans Picture Library 28 (both); the Hutchison Library 8, 39 (top), 41 (top), 44; Photoresources 11 (bottom); Rex Features 45 (top); Sefton Picture Library *frontispiece*, 35 (below); Spectrum Colour Library 24 (top); Topham Picture Library 12, 13, 42; ZEFA Picture Library *cover*, 5; Wayland Picture Library 10, 22, 23 (both), 30 (left).

Index